THE PATH TO *VICTORY*

8 STEPS TO POSSESS THE LAND THAT GOD HAS GIVEN YOU...

THE PATH TO *VICTORY*

8 STEPS TO POSSESS THE LAND THAT GOD HAS GIVEN YOU...

JERRY BONSU

Copyright © 2013 Jerry Bonsu

All rights reserved. No part of this publication may be reproduced without the written permission of the publisher, with the exception of brief excerpts in magazines, articles, reviews, etc.

THE PATH TO VICTORY

Published in France by VICTORY LIFE MEDIA an imprint of JBM

JERRY BONSU MINISTRIES
http://www.jerrybonsu.org
E-mail: info@jerrybonsu.org

French National Library-in-Publication Data
Dépôt légal: 11/2013

Original and modified cover art by Minoru Nitta and CoverDesignStudio.com

Editing by Scott Philip Stewart (CAS)

Printed in the USA

ISBN: 978-2-9541960-2-2

Unless otherwise noted, Scripture quotations are from the New King James Version of the Bible. King James Version © 1982 by Thomas Nelson, Inc. New International Version of the Bible.

For further information or permission, contact us on the Internet:

VICTORY LIFE MEDIA *"Empowering our Generation for the next Generation"* www.victorylifemedia.com

It Is TIME to POSSESS the LAND !

Every place that the sole of your foot shall tread upon, that have I given unto you...
Joshua 1:3

CONTENTS

INTRODUCTION : It Is Time To Possess The Land 9

STEP 1   Be Strong And Courageous 15

STEP 2   Define Your Territory! 21

STEP 3   Identify The Obstacles 25

STEP 4   Stand! You Are Not Alone 31

STEP 5   Know Your Weapons 37

STEP 6   Take a Step Of Faith 49

STEP 7   Embrace God's Divine Strategy 55

STEP 8   Make a Joyful Noise! 61

CONCLUSION : Your Path To Victory 75
   * Thoughts & Reflections.................................... 79
   * Bibliography ……………….................................. 93
   * About The Author 95

Introduction

IT IS TIME TO POSSESS THE LAND

I ENJOY JOURNEYS. I love visiting new places. So following the Lord has been a great adventure for me because it is the path of faith, fight, and victory. There is no victory without a battle. *Never forget that.* God has called His people to live on the mountaintop and to experience all the blessings, possessions, and purposes of His design. But on the way to that mountaintop, you must fight – climb over some rocky terrain and negotiate some steep passes.

If you are a believer and a follower of the Lord, God has bigger and brighter things for your life than you have ever imagined.

One day as I was reading the final edit of my book *PUSH*, which talks about the power of praise, prayer and persistence, the Holy Spirit led me to the chapter 8, "Your Path to Victory," and asked me to take some notes. Yes, this might seem strange. Why would God ask me to take notes from my own book? Maybe you have felt the same way at times when God asked you to revisit some familiar territory. I even asked God, "Is this really *You* speaking?" Then the Lord took me to Joshua 1:1-3 (RSV):

> *"After the death of Moses the servant of the Lord, it came to pass that the Lord spoke to Joshua the son of Nun, Moses' assistant, saying: 'Moses My servant is dead. Now therefore, arise, go over this Jordan,*

THE PATH TO VICTORY

you and all this people, to the land which I am giving to them – the children of Israel. Every place that the sole of your foot will tread upon I have given you, as I said to Moses."

Through this passage, God spoke to my heart about His plan for this generation. He said to me, "It is time to possess the land." At that moment I understood that God was about to release a divine strategy. He was about to show me the pathway from slavery to freedom just as He had the children of Israel. So I began to take notes. As I continued writing, something amazing happened. What God showed me that day is what I'm about to share with you in this book. In fact, I am about to introduce to you a radically different approach to life that will ultimately lead you to your divine destination.

God wants to bring each of us into our promised land. This promised land is not a geographic location but a land where His promises are being fulfilled in our lives. It is a place of prosperity, blessing, and fruitfulness designed to move us to glorify Him.

But before we start our journey, let me ask you a few questions: *What has God promised you? What has He spoken to your heart? Are you counting on Him to keep His promises? Do you believe that God has a plan for your life? Have you ever thought about what it takes to have a happy, successful, fulfilled life? Why do some people seem to have a victorious life, a good and abundant life, while others seem to live in a world of "whatever happens, happens"?*

I want you to know this: There is a promised land for you personally, and God wants to lead you to it. God wants you to live a victorious life. God wants you to possess the

Introduction

land, which is your inheritance in Christ. Our Heavenly Father wants His children – that is you and me – to be blessed during our lives on earth. He doesn't want us to just wade through life until we go to heaven. He created the earth—the beauty, the trees, the animals, the food – for *us*, all for our enjoyment. In fact, He cares deeply for us and in concerned with how we live and our quality of life. God wants to give us everything.

The Scriptures tell us that "blessed are the people who know the joyful sound! They walk, O LORD, in the light of Your countenance. In Your name they rejoice all day long, And in Your righteousness they are exalted" (Psalm 89:15-16). This is God's desire for us Christians. He wants His people to be free from all worldly concerns and from things that weigh us down. When we are lifted above the circumstances of life and rejoice all day long, no matter how difficult things may be, we become valuable tools and weapons in the hand of God. We become effective warriors who are able to take the kingdom by force. This is God's plan and design for us! But…

On the other hand, we have an enemy who wants to keep us in check. Every time we start to rejoice and walk in the light of God's countenance, the enemy will do his best to shut us up and cause us to stumble. He will try to keep us in a state of misery, discouragement, hopelessness, depression, and whatever other adversity he can throw at us, because he wants us to be ineffective warriors for the cause of Christ.

Satan is the accuser of the brethren and will throw at us everything he can get away with. He does not want us to know the joyful sound and to walk in the light of God's countenance. But the good news is that *God wants you to win*

THE PATH TO VICTORY

In fact, He has already given you the victory over the enemy! He said:

> *"I have given you authority to trample on snakes and scorpions and to overcome all the power of the enemy; nothing will harm you."*
>
> Luke 10:19

Many of us see God's promises right before us. But when we see the giants that we must defeat in order to possess them, we shrink, retreat, and give up. Many of us think that we are destined to fail. We sometimes even label ourselves as "failures." As a result, we go through life forever searching for answers to the big questions "What am I here for?" and "Which path should I take?" when *God has already provided the answers.*

In Joshua 1:2, God told Joshua, "Arise." When you begin to see yourself as God sees you, and believe that you can do all things through Christ who strengthens you (Philippians 4:13), you will ARISE in faith, ARISE in expectation, ARISE in your authority in Christ! Part of the process of possessing your promised land and being successful is to recognize that *you* have a part to play.

So many people "wait on God" to take them to their Place of fulfillment in life and then blame Him when they fail to get there. Some even think God will magically fix their situation. Friend, here's a news flash: *God isn't into magic tricks!* He has a master plan, and your job is to operate within that plan. It is time to possess the land – whatever the land that is set before you is. It is time to possess it!

The Bible says; "there is a time for everything under the

Introduction

sun, a time to be born and a time to die, a time to laugh and a time to cry" (See Ecclesiastes 3). Well now is the time to possess the land. The land is set before you and just as His Word came to Jeremiah, Joshua, and Moses, so also His Word has come to you today. Though the land I am talking about is your spiritual inheritance in Christ Jesus, it doesn't remain spiritual and intangible. On the contrary, it is tangible! Rise up and possess it, for the time is now! You have tarried long enough. You have delayed way too long. You have looked out at the sky and read the weather to know what time it is. Well the time is now! The time to possess your Canaan (promised land) is here! I encourage you to rise up and defy all odds and possess that land.

Friend, this is the season to overcome the giants at Jericho. For God has a plans for you, "plans to prosper you and not to harm you, plans to give you hope and a future" (Jeremiah 29:11). There is a tangible promotion, a tangible business opportunity, a tangible healing, a tangible expansion, a tangible manifestation of the blessing waiting for you. *Rejoice!* For you are about to discover God's plan for your life and identify the process that will lead you to possess your promised land (your divine destination) that flows with milk and honey.

The goal of this book is to help you gain a greater awareness of that process and the factors that lead to your desired end. I will guide you step-by-step through the process you can take to possess your inheritance in Christ, achieve success, enrich your life, and discover your life's purpose.

I encourage you to open your heart and mind to the new direction that God is leading you. No matter where you are today – and regardless of the decisions you made yesterday

THE PATH TO VICTORY

– know that there is hope. Today is a new day filled with opportunity. Get ready because your whole way of thinking is about to change.

If you are ready to experience God's best, and walk out His plan for your life, get a pen and some paper and let's take this journey together. The promised land is for you NOW! Step into it!!!

STEP 1

BE STRONG AND COURAGEOUS

Have I not commanded you? Be strong and courageous. Do not be terrified, do not be discouraged, for the Lord your God will be with you wherever you go."

Joshua 1:9

MOSES HAD JUST SPENT 40 years leading the Israelites through the wilderness. He was the only man to talk to God face to face (Exodus 33:11). He was a great leader and man of God, but his time was up. He was to pass the reins to a new leader who would lead God's people to the Promised Land. This man was Joshua. In the first nine verses of Joshua chapter 1 God gives Joshua a pep talk in preparation for his task.

As you read the pep talk, note that there is one thing that God mentions over and over: "BE STRONG AND COURAGEOUS." In verse 9, God says this for the third time, but that is not all. Before Moses died, he told Joshua twice to "be strong and courageous" (Deuteronomy 31:6-7). And again, when the Lord commissioned Joshua, He told him to "be strong and courageous" (Deuteronomy 31:23). And then the people of Israel respond by charging Joshua to "be strong and courageous" (Joshua 1:18).

The question is: Why is the exhortation to "be strong and courageous" repeated so many times? Why do we need to be strong and of good courage to possess the land that

THE PATH TO VICTORY

God our Father in heaven has given to us on this earth?

First: When God gives you a promise...you fight for it! Joshua was going to need strength and courage to take the land. The good news is that God had given Him the land. The bad news was that He gave it to someone else -- at first. Joshua was facing a land of walled cities, and to make matters worse, he had no siege engines.

Have you ever given up on a promise because it never seemed to come to pass or because you lacked the financial resources to accomplish a God-given vision? That can seem very discouraging, which is why God told Joshua to be strong and of good courage, not wimpy and discouraged.

If God tells you that you will have victory, then stand on that promise! If He says everything you touch will be abundant you must stand and fight for the promise even if everything you touch seems to fall apart! If He says a loved one will be healed, you fight and don't let the "father of lies" (Satan) have his way! Whose report shall you believe – God's Word or a doctor's word?

There is no victory without a battle.

We can let fear dominate our life or we can choose to be strong and courageous. I say we can *choose*, but have you noticed from the above verse that it is not given as an option but rather as a command? Why would God do that? Why would He command us to be strong and courageous? Because we NEED it and He is WORTHY of it! Of course we do have options to disobey the command. We can let fear grip our heart and influence our decisions. We can rationalize and make excuses for why we can't be strong or courageous. We can justify why we should be discouraged and drown in self-pity. But as we do, let's not forget what

Be strong and courageous

God commands: "Do not be terrified, do not be discouraged, for the Lord your God will be with you wherever you go."

Friend, courage is required for overcoming the challenges of life. If Joshua had looked at the giants in the land and based his decisions on the circumstances around him, he and all who followed him would never have made it to their promise.

You see, God's word stands true and He fulfills *every* promise despite the problems we face. Where you are today is not your final destination but only a place of preparation for what is to come. So when the onslaught of hell comes against you to take you out, fight back! Stand on the word of God! When the enemy creeps in to tell you how unworthy you are, fight back! And stand upon the promise that you are a blood-bought child of the Most High God!

Don't let your heart be troubled by the problems of this world. Keep your eyes on Christ and focus on what is true and right. The lies of the enemy have no power to steal your joy, so do not willingly give it up to him. Hold on to the heritage that you have because of what Christ sacrificed for us.

No matter what the situation looks like, seek the Lord and stand upon His Word. Seeking the Lord's heart will save you from fighting battles that you were never supposed to fight and keep you fighting for the honor of your Lord and Savior. For He is worthy!

> When God gives you a promise... you fight for it!

Second: It takes courage to obey God when everybody else isn't. Though it is not easy to obey God when you are surrounded by others who are, it takes great courage to obey God as a visionary and to condemn sin when public opinion says it's okay.

God told Joshua to be strong and courageous because he would have to obey God's law. Many Christians spend far too much time trying to discern God's will for their lives. This plays itself out in a stutter-step life punctuated by stops at every intersection in life to cast their lots or wait for a word from God. How many times has God given you this pep talk and told you to be "strong and courageous" and yet you become timid and cowardly based on the advice your receive from those around you.

Remember, Joshua was one of only two men who said God could help them take the promised land when the other 10 were afraid (Numbers 13:30). Let your faith stand in the power of God and not in the wisdom of men. Why? Because the wisdom of men can leave you pretty jacked up.

1 Corinthians 2:5 says:

> *"That your faith should not stand in the wisdom of men, but in the power of God. "*

God is forever faithful! He cannot disappoint or fail you because He is God! He keeps every covenant He has ever made. Every one of His promises and foretellings either already has or will come true. God's faithfulness is borne out in testimony after testimony of His people in the scriptures, and His people today still give testimonies of His unfailing faithfulness.

In fact, we find some 277 accounts of covenants God entered into with His people in the Bible. Deuteronomy 7:9 says: *"Know therefore that the LORD your God is God; he is the*

Be strong and courageous

faithful God, keeping his covenant of love to a thousand generations of those who love him and keep his commandments."

Believe that God has a plan for your life. He is calling you to do great things just as He called Caleb to do great things. Note that God did not tell Joshua to take it slow and to pray over every little detail. He didn't tell him to seek the counsel of 3-5 godly men before making any decision. He told him to be "strong and courageous."

God sees what you are going through. He knows all of your problems, and He is telling you, "I am with you. I will not leave you nor forsake you. Every place that the sole of your foot will tread upon I have given you!"

> It takes courage to obey God when everybody else isn't.

Don't let fear stop you from doing what God is telling you to do. Just as He did with Joshua, God has already set in your heart what you have to do and *He wants you to do it now!* Just be strong and courageous! Never, ever give up! Go out and possess the land the Lord has given you for His honor, and for His glory!

Today, may the Lord give you the courage of Joshua and Caleb – courage to believe you can possess your possessions, conquer your Canaan, and enter into what God has for you in Jesus' name!

STEP 2

DEFINE YOUR TERRITORY!

"Your territory will extend from the desert to Lebanon, and from the great river, the Euphrates – all the Hittite country – to the Great Sea on the west."

Joshua 1:4

WITHOUT A VISION the people perish. God gave Joshua not only a clear vision but a promise of fulfilment: *"...cross the Jordan River into the land I am about to give them..."* God then went on to define the extent of that land: *"Your territory will extend from the desert to Lebanon, and from the great river, the Euphrates – all the Hittite country – to the Great Sea on the west."* And He said to Joshua: *"Every place that the sole of your foot shall tread upon, that have I given unto you, as I said unto Moses."* The prophetic is manifest through the natural world. God uses the "soles of the feet" to represent possessing. Jesus told His disciples that they would tread on serpents with their feet (Luke 10:19). The feet represent possessing and taking territory.

"How blessed on the mountain are the feet of them who bring good tidings of great joy."
Isaiah 52:7

The children of Israel knew all about the feet. Their shoes had not worn out during the 40 years they spent wandering in the wilderness, and now the same feet that had wandered through the desert were about to take the land. *"As I said to Moses...."* Again and again God reaffirms His Word to our hearts.

When God promises something, He knows the exact size of that promise. He has in mind everything that He wants to give us through that promise. The conjunction of God's command to get ready to cross over into the promised land with His precise description of the land tells us that there is always a promise to be wholly claimed. Before claiming your promises, however, you must define your territory! Until you have a clear understanding of what God has promised to give you, you cannot take it. Evangeslit Reinhard Bonnke could not move forward until God gave him a vision of a blood-bought Africa. He has now preached to over 1 million souls at a single crusade!

> *"And the Lord answered me and said, Write the vision and engrave it so plainly upon the tablets that everyone who passes may [be able to] read [it easily and quickly] as he hastens by"*
> Habakkuk 2:2 (AMP)

In other words, the Lord said, "Write down what I tell you. Do not sugar coat it, do not add to it. Just make it plain as the light of day. I want you to engrave it in such clarity that you and anyone else who may be passing by can look up see it and read it easily and quickly."

Brothers and sisters, the vision is given to you in order that you may know the truth. How many times in your life has God provided you with a vision that you just cast aside saying, "This is just another one of those pie-in-the-sky dre-

Define your territory!

ams I had that will never come true?" Listen up: The time has come in your life for you to believe in what God is showing you and to see it for what it truly is – the right vision for the right time.

Write down the territory that God has given you: Your gifts, your family and household of influence, your business, your ministry calling, your integrity and character. All of these are your areas of territory. They are your promised land, given to you by almighty God, and now you must take it.

> *When God promises something, He knows the exact size of that promise.*

Write down the revelation and make it plain! Write it down in bold print with a permanent marker and tack it up on the walls of your home. Hang the list on your car visor. Put it on your desk at work. Memorize it. It is your territory! Run with it. It is your promised land! You will fulfill your destiny. You will die with satisfaction, knowing that you enjoyed the abundant (rich and full) life that Jesus promised you, certain that you finished the race and fought the good fight.

When you close your eyes for the last time on this earth you will hear the sweet words echoing in the distance, "Well done thou good and faithful servant." Your family will have a blessed legacy of knowing what your territory was and that you completed your work.

Friend, the territory that God wants you to take possession of is a place of promise for you, a place of potential, perhaps unrealised, yet possible! It is a place of adventure, of vision, of desire, of dreaming. It is a place full of excitement and new challenges. There are giants to def-

THE PATH TO VICTORY

eat – great giants, but the blessings are all the greater. You would do well right this minute to sit down and list them. Know who you are in Christ. Know what He has given you and stand on it. Take it – take it all – and don't take no for an answer.

You will fulfill your destiny.

It is time to define that place and defend it! It is the time to go out and possess the land!

STEP 3

IDENTIFY THE OBSTACLES

"...Today you are on the verge of battle with your enemies. Do not let your heart faint, do not be afraid, and do not tremble or be terrified because of them;"

Joshua 6 :1-2

TAKING POSSESSION of the promised land will always entail obstacles. Obstacles are barriers or restrictions that we run up against along life's path. Some obstacles we jump over, some we go around, some we knock down, and some take great energy and effort to conquer. We all face tests of our faith. Many times when we encounter an obstacle or face a trial in our life, our goal is to remove it, to get rid of it, to leap over it with a single bound!

But have you every paused to consider that maybe that obstacle serves a greater purpose than just being a hurdle in the race of life? The truth is, seeing and understanding the obstacles can actually help us. Jesus talked about counting the costs. Before we launch out on a new venture, for instance, we must count the costs. This means we consider the investment it will take and decide whether we are willing to pay the price. God gave the people of Israel a grand promise – *The Promised Land* that was flowing with milk and honey.

Yet the journey to get to it was not easy. There were many tests as they wandered through the wilderness. They faced both natural and physical obstacles, such as the Red

Sea, the barren desert (no water, no food), and the Jordan River. If all that wasn't enough, the promised land Canaan was teeming with enemies and giants who were living there and called it *their* home.

After a very long and difficult journey the Israelites had finally reached the border of their promised land. They were but one step away. God's leading and care through the rigors of the wilderness had been great. He had provided for all their needs. The new generation was about to enter the land.

There remained but one last barrier – the River Jordan. To reach the promised land, they had only to cross it. Their previous generation, their fathers and grandfathers, had experienced God's parting of the Red Sea as the children of Israel fled the slavery of Pharaoh. Now this new generation was about to experience God's power in their own way. He was going to lead them across the River Jordan.

> Taking possession of the promised land will always entail obstacles.

Notice how in the Old Testament the people of Israel recalled key events of their history and particularly the Exodus, their journey out of Egypt, very often (even in the Psalms). It was through this journey that they first experienced God's awesome power and unfailing faithfulness. This historical experience was important. They were able to trust God today because they had seen God's power and faithfulness in the past. Though they knew the obstacles that stood in their way, they still carried on with the journey and stood upon the Word of God and walked closer and closer to the river.

Identify the obstacles

"Dear brothers and sisters, when troubles come your way, consider it an opportunity for great joy. For you know that when your faith is tested, your endurance has a chance to grow. So let it grow, for when your endurance is fully developed, you will be perfect and complete, needing nothing."
James 1:2-4 (NLT)

According to James, we are not to greet trials and obstacles and hurdles with a desire to get around them or overcome them. Rather, we are to accept them with great joy! God often uses obstacles to teach us, to truly make us stronger, and to give us a skill set that we could get in no other way. Romans 8:28 says, "For God works all things for the good of those who love Him." That is *all* things — both good and bad.

So even as we follow God's will in this life, we can expect to encounter obstacles, setbacks, enemies, and heartaches. But we know that we will have the final victory because God works these negative circumstances for our *good*. See whatever trials and adversity are in front of you for what they are: tests of your "faith muscle." They cause you to become stronger. You can call them your Gold's Gym of spiritual living.

So take a look at the obstacle in front of you and ask yourself: *How is it testing my faith? Is it making me rely more upon God? Is it causing me to depend on Him more? Have I spent time on my knees asking Him to show me what He wants me to learn spiritually through this?*

Until you understand the nature of the trial and its purpose from a kingdom perspective, you will never be *able* to overcome the obstacle in the right way and can never truly have a victorious life. If you allow the Lord to change your perspective, then you can look upon those obstacles as opportunities, trials as testings, adversity as advancement! Whatever obstacles you are facing today, God will use them to promote you. He will use your enemies to show forth His power.

Obstacles can sometimes also be distractions that Satan uses to sway believers from their purpose. Once you make a decision to obey God and walk in faith, the enemy can do nothing with you but distract you from the purpose God has called you.

It is obvious that so many believers are growing weary in these dark days of oppression that we live. Struggles surround us at every corner and it is hard to stave off the growing fears of uncertainty. We were told in Scripture that these times would come and test the faithful, but how do we keep standing when the ground is trembling and darkness is filling the sky? There are many times in our lives when the obstacles in front of us might seem insurmountable. We may be tempted to think that we can't go on; that we cannot possibly achieve our goals and we might as well just turn around and quit. Today, your barrier may not be a river just like the Israelites. Maybe a bad habit, an addiction, an attitude... maybe it's a difficulty at work, or in your family. Some kind

> *If you allow the Lord to change your perspective, then you can look upon those obstacles as opportunities, trials as testings, adversity as advancement!*

Identify the obstacles

of barrier that stops you from being at the place God wants you to be, or being the person God meant you to be. But you can overcome! God said; *"Today I will begin to exalt you in the eyes of all..., so they may know that I am with you..."* Let God change your perception and see yourself as He sees you! Look up to Jesus, and not the obstacles! Take the "next right step" in obedience and declare; *"I can do all things through Christ who strengthens me."* (Philippians 4:13)

> Look up to Jesus, and not the obstacles!

Joshua and the people of Israel walking toward the river that day could have felt like quitting. They might have been tempted to turn around and go back to Egypt (The world) or stay in the wilderness (Period of dryness), but instead they kept on walking toward their promised land (Divine destination), a land flowing with milk and honey.

When life's obstacles seem too great for you to deal with, that is what you must do as well. Instead of quitting, you must keep walking toward God's promises. You must step out in faith because of your love for Jesus, and leave everything else to God. You must trust Him to help you along the way to overcome whatever obstacles life throws at you.

The Isrealites didn't know how their journey was going to turn out, but they knew that the one thing they could control was what they chose to do that day, so they chose to keep walking toward the promised land. We don't know how our journey is going to turn out either, but we can keep walking toward the dream, the vision, the purpose and trust that when we come to our expected obstacle we will find that God has already overcome it.

THE PATH TO VICTORY

In this battle, you are a winner! You are an overcomer! You are more than a conqueror! Praise God! —For the obstacles is only here to develop strength.

Remind yourself of the promises, and prophetic words that God has spoken over your life. For this prophetic declarations that are spoken over your life will become one of the greatest weapons through the battles.

Today, trust God. He will grant you the resources to overcome your obstacles and reach your destination.

STEP 4

STAND! YOU ARE NOT ALONE

"...I will be with you; I will never leave you nor forsake you."

Joshua 6 :5

As SOMEONE SAID; It does not matter where you are in your life; it only matters where God is going to take you. God's light is our solace in a lost and perishing world.

The word of God promises us that we will have peace despite our situation and that He has a plan to give us a future with hope. Jesus has paid the price for our victory in every circumstance. There is never a battle that can defeat you. It is only when you understand that you are more than a conqueror through Jesus Christ that you can believe that God's strength and His perfect plan for your life are all that you need.

God has helped some of the most unlikely people to be victors in the spiritual battles we all face! He has used ordinary people to do extraordinary things. Now, why would He do that? It's because God wants to display His power, His glory and who He is to everyone everywhere. And He wants to use you and I to do display that power. Which brings to ask these questions; How does God pick people to fight great battles for Him? What is it that God looks for when looking for a

> *I will never leave you nor forsake you.*

champion? Does He look for great talents, great minds, great abilities, great standing in society, great pedigrees, or great names?

Why did God pick a deceitful Jacob? Why did God pick Abel over Cain? Why did God pick David over Saul? Why did God pick a farmer like Amos over a trained prophet? Why did God pick a Moses who by his own admission couldn't speak well? Why did God pick sickly and fearful Timothy? Why did God pick a shaky and fearful Gideon who by anyone's standards was severely insecure?

- **Joshua**, a brilliant military commander needed to "Be strong and very courageous". He responded to God's promise and command with absolute faith. And step out to possess the promised land.
- **Jacob** was deceitful because he wanted more than anything else God's blessings! He was committed to getting from God the best!
- **Abel** was committed to being obedient to God's Word about proper sacrifices!
- **David** was more concerned about God's name than his own!
- **Amos**' only concern was to see God's people experience revival!
- **Moses** made some serious mistakes, but he wanted so much to see God's people released from bondage!
- **Timothy**, Paul said there was no one like-minded more than Timothy, in spite of his frailties and frequent illnesses and timidity. Paul says he demonstrated a faithfulness like few others in his day, both to Paul as a senior partner, and to the church of Jesus Christ!

Stand! You are not alone

Each of these men had serious flaws, but there were some things they had in common that made them candidates for God's help in battle: They were committed to God and His people! They were wiling to serve no matter the resistance, they were quick to repent when shown their own wrong, they were concerned more about others than themselves, they were faithful in spite of setbacks, and they were not quitters though at times they felt like quitting! They were willing to overcome their own faults to put God first, and God's people above themselves. Their character was something God found solid.

> God's strength and His perfect plan for your life are all that you need.

In other words, God found in these flawed men characteristics that ministry could be built on! Something great can be done with them! God would help hone their skills, it was their character however that enabled God to be with them in battle! God promises to be with us in battle when our hearts are in the right place, we need not fear being overcome by the enemy; God will fight with us, for us, and through us!

In Isaiah 59:19 the Bible says;

"When the enemy comes in like a flood, The Spirit of the Lord will lift up a standard against him."

Yes! The enemy will certainly comes in like a flood, for the territory we fight for is mostly spiritual and realms of authority. But the Scripture assures us, the Lord will stand up against the *enemy* (satan and his minions) when he comes in like a raging flood, condemning and accusing and trying to push us down and under, and to cause us to be overcome and overwhelmed.

Brothers and Sisters, the storms of life are going to come; but don't let them disturb your peace and effect your thoughts and emotions. The battle you are facing is most likely a battle for territory. Even though your victory is certain, as long as you continue you will face opposition.

> God will fight with us, for us, and through us!

The devil would like you to quit or to turn back or to be distracted. You must not be distracted. STAND! Stay focused and keep the right attitude!!! —Have an attitude of praise! An obedient attitude, a thankful attitude, and a joyful attitude! Trust God for all that would follow crossing into the new territory. Yes! There would be giants to slay, but God is the commander in chief, the Captain of the Lord's Host. (Joshua 5:13-15). He will pull you through. I challenge you today to take the mighty weapons God has given you and get into the battle!

"For we do not wrestle against flesh and blood, but against principalities, against powers, against the rulers of the darkness of this age, against spiritual hosts of wickedness in the heavenly places."

Ephesians 6:12

Nothing can overcome you when your life is in Christ. He is your power and the force to go on even despite the pain you may be experiencing. God is never limited by the impossibility of your situation. He who spoke the world into existence has a way out of every trial you endure. In Scripture we read that it was God who shut the mouth of the lions and saved Daniel when he was thrown into their den for not bowing down to the king. It was God who went with young David to defeat the giant. It is always the strength of God who meets us at the battle and takes down our enemies. We have nothing to fear because the word of God promises us that we cannot be destroyed.

> Trust God for all that would follow crossing into the new territory.

It is time to be aggressive and energetic when it comes to letting go of the past and pressing forward to the abundant life God has in store for you. It is time to rise up and boldly go after your victory! It is time to develop a warrior mentality and proactively pursue the happiness, health, and peace that God has promised in His Word. *"The God of all grace who called you to his eternal glory in Christ, after you have suffered a little while, will himself restore you and make you strong, firm and steadfast."* (1 Peter 5:10). The storms that this life brings will be turned around for your good and will bring you to the knowledge of how wide and long and high and deep is the love of Christ. (Ephesians 3:18).

Friend, understand this; "It is only after you have been in a painful battle and watched as your God defeated all of your problems that you can grow in unwavering trust. If God is for us, who can be against us? (Romans 8:31).

Now, let's go to the next step and see some of the weapons of our warfare.

STEP 5

KNOW YOUR WEAPONS

"For the weapons of our warfare are not of the flesh, but divinely powerful for the destruction of fortresses "

2 Corinthians 10:4 (NASB)

THE APOSTLE PAUL here states that we are engaged in a warfare – spiritual warfare – and must use various weapons to fight. Guns, knives, and bombs are effective against the enemies that we can see in the physical realm but have no power against those we cannot see in the spiritual realm. As Paul states in Ephesians 6:12, our fight is not with flesh and blood (with people) but with the host of demons that work to defile, destroy, harass, tempt, and enslave mankind.

Part of the good news (the Gospel) of Jesus Christ is that now we can not only resist the devil's influence in our own lives but we can destroy his influence in the lives of others. God has given us mighty weapons to counter satanic influence and activity. To be effective in our warfare, however, we must know what these weapons are and how to use them effectively.

Friend, there is a fierce war raging on! The Holy Spirit has given us a powerful spiritual tools we can use as a weapons against the wiles of the enemy and the giants occupying our promised land. The question is: Are you using all the weapons in your spiritual arsenal? It is up to you to pick up the weapons and learn how to use them. If you follow your natural tendency and wait for a crisis before taking up your weapons, your lack of skill will surely be exposed in defeat.

The enemy is a highly skilled adversary. Satan's spiritual forces are experienced veterans, having waged war on mankind for thousands of years. They know our weaknesses and how best to exploit them. God calls us to be good warriors, trained and skilled in using the weapons He has given us. The Apostle Paul said we are engaged in spiritual warfare and have the weapons we need to overcome Satan's strongholds.

> *"The weapons we fight with are not the weapons of the world. On the contrary, they have divine power to demolish strongholds. We demolish arguments and every pretension that sets itself up against the knowledge of God, and we take captive every thought to make it obedient to Christ."*
> 2 Corinthians 10:4-5

Many Christians often wonder why they are still struggling with a myriad of issues, although they have been saved and born again through Christ. Why are so many of us are still living with illness and disease, addiction, fear and anxiety, depression, emotional scars, negative childhood memories, and more? I have often said that it is not always about what we are doing wrong. Sometimes it is that we are not doing enough of what is right.

The fact is, in the natural fallen world we live in, we will still have to struggle against many spiritual attacks, weaknesses of the flesh, strongholds, and negative mindsets

Know your weapons

. And during certain periods of difficulties we must use the extra defense, inspiration, and intervention that comes from the power of the Holy Spirit within. In other words: to overcome certain barriers to our victory through Christ, we must be prepared to engage in spiritual warfare! We must know our weapons and how to use them! The keys I am about to share with you are eternally vital and life-transforming strategies for overcoming the challenges of life.

Separately, I believe each is as important to the believer as eating or drinking. But when combined they cleanse, purify, and prepare the believer for battle—and fill us to overflowing with the power of God's Spirit. They are spiritual weapons that will help you break generational curses, overcome bad habits and negative self-talk, and achieve the true freedom that God intends for you.

> *It is up to you to pick up the weapons and learn how to use them.*

Here are the weapons (keys) that will prepare you to battle your obstacles through spiritual warfare.

• PRAISE

Praise is a major weapon against Satan. He and his demons just hate hearing people praise God, especially when they do so from a pure heart. Praise releases the presence of God in a way that the enemy cannot resist. If you will praise God more, you will have far less interference from demonic powers in your life. Praise silences the enemy!

THE PATH TO VICTORY

The Bible says:

*"Out of the mouths of babes and nursing infants
You have ordained strength, because of your
enemies, that you may silence the enemy and the
avenger."* (Psalm 8:2)

Jesus also confirmed this in Matthew 21:16 when He said, "Yes, have you never read, 'Out of the mouth of babes and nursing infants you have perfected praise.'" The strength that God has ordained for you is perfect praise. Perfect praise SILENCES the enemy and the avenger. Many of your problems would be solved if you could only get Satan and his demons to SHUT UP!

The battle you have to fight today is in your mind. The enemy and his demons operate by injecting suggestions into your mind that *seem* plausible but are rooted in unbelief and rebellion against God. The suggestions appear to be your own thoughts, when they are not at all! When you believe and trust these demonic suggestions – and take them as your own – you lose battles.

> Praise silences the enemy!

These suggestions, thoughts, and imaginations work to sow discouragement, confusion, fear, doubt, and unbelief in your minds. You have to change your thinking in order to possess God's promises. Start choosing thoughts of faith and victory. Declare through praise that you are an overcomer. As you stand and fight and win the battle in your mind, you will move forward and embrace the promises and dreams that God has for you!

In my book *PUSH*, I explain how perfect praise led by

Know your weapons

God's Holy Spirit will completely silence the enemy and his demons. Here is one reason why you should consider how you might praise God better. The Bible provides many exhortations to the people of God to praise God. We can find these in the Psalms. Shouting, dancing, singing, rejoicing, and making music are all valid biblical ways of expressing praise to God. God dwells manifestly by His Spirit in the PRAISES OF HIS PEOPLE. The psalmist said, "But You are holy, enthroned on the praises of Israel" (Psalm 22:3).

The Kingdom of God will manifest through the presence of the King, which comes when we praise Him. The manifest presence of God drives demons OUT of the places near us where they can seek to gain influence over us. Let us therefore praise the Lord now more than ever before!

On one occasion, Jehoshophat, the King of Israel, came against a vast opposing army of many nations bent on Israel's destruction (2 Chronicles 20). The King put at the front lines of the army people who PRAISED the LORD with singing saying, "Praise the LORD, for His mercy endures forever." And the Bible says, "As they began to sing and praise, the Lord set ambushes against the men of Ammon and Moab and Mount Seir who were invading Judah, and they were defeated."

It is no accident that David, perhaps the mightiest warrior for God in Old Testament times, was a man of praise. His strength was rooted in the joy he gave God through praising and worshiping God. How much more are we – you and I in these New Testament times who are commanded to possess the land, "continually offer up to God the sacrifice of praise, the fruit of lips which confess His Name" (Hebrews 13:15) – called to overcome the devil

THE PATH TO VICTORY

and his demons and all their works using PRAISE as a mighty God-ordained weapon for the destruction of their plans and works.

• THE WORD OF GOD

"Take the helmet of salvation and the sword of the Spirit, which is the word of God."

Ephesians 6:17

The Word of God is both a defensive weapon and an offensive weapon. It is incredibly powerful and effective at driving away the enemy and tearing down his work. It is living and active, sharper than any double-edged sword, and penetrates even to dividing soul and spirit, joints and marrow; it judges the thoughts and attitudes of the heart (Hebrews 4:12). Paul referred to it as "The sword of the Spirit." When Jesus was tempted by Satan in the wilderness (Luke 4:1-13), He overcame the devil using one weapon – THE WORD OF GOD.

> The battle you have to fight today is in your mind.

Rather than arguing directly with Satan's suggestions, as many of us try to do, Jesus simply quoted the Word of God as it applied to the suggestion. When Satan tried to suggest a course of action for Jesus to prove His divinity and simultaneously satisfy His hunger, Jesus answered, "It is written, 'Man shall not live by bread alone, but by every word of God" (Luke 4:4). This silenced the enemy and ended the discussion on that point. Jesus used the Word of God once for each of the three main temptations that every son of man must face. These are:

- **The lust of the flesh**
- **The lust of the eyes**
- **The pride of life**

"Do not love the world or the things in the world. If anyone loves the world, the love of the Father is not in him. For all that is in the world - the lust of the flesh, the lust of the eyes, and the pride of life - is not of the Father but is of the world. And the world is passing away, and the lust of it; but he who does the will of God abides forever."
1 John 2:15-17

Once we have overcome these fully, we have overcome Satan. The Apostle John wrote, "I have written to you, young men, because you are strong, and the Word of God abides in you, and you have overcome the wicked one" (1 John 2:14). We see then that we are called to grow up to the stage of being "young men" in whom the Word of God abides so that we are "no longer children, tossed about by every wind and wave of doctrine" (Ephesians 4:14).

Only when, through much study and meditation on the Word of God, the word comes to live in us and consumes our thoughts will we be strong in the Lord. Jesus promised that if we abide in Him, and His Word abides in us, we will ask what we desire and it will be done for us (John 15:7). This will include victory over Satan.

The Word of God protects our vital organs (spiritually speaking). It protects our hearts and our emotions as we walk with God. The Word of God protects our minds from the onslaughts of Satan and his wicked thoughts. The Word of God is our offensive weapon to aggressively fight against spiritual wickedness. So how can we fight against Satan if we don't know the Word of God? We cannot! It is impossible!

Jesus Himself was our example in using "the whole armour of God," the holy Word of God, to fight against Satan when He said, "Get thee behind me, Satan: for it is written, Thou shalt worship the Lord thy God, and him only shalt thou serve" (Luke 4:8). When we know the Word of God, we learn that we are "heirs of God, and joint-heirs with Christ" (Romans 8:17), and that we should put on the Lord Jesus Christ, and make no provision for the flesh to fulfil the lusts thereof. We are supposed to present our "bodies a living sacrifice, holy, acceptable unto God," which is our reasonable service, and we should not be conformed to this world but rather be transformed by the renewing of our mind, that we may prove what is that good, and acceptable, and perfect, will of God (Romans 12:1-2).

• PRAYER

Someone said, "Prayer is not preparation for the battle. Prayer *is* the battle." The Bible commands us to pray without ceasing, so we should at least aim for it. God has made so many promises regarding prayer, and we need to fill our hearts and minds with these promises. Prayer is how we communicate with our Commander-in-Chief, the Lord Jesus Christ, so that we can receive our marching orders and know how to proceed. According to the Word of God, prayer is also the means by which we communicate orders in the spiritual world. We are promised that whatever we ask for in prayer, believing, we will receive. "Therefore I tell you, whatever you ask for in prayer, believe that you have received it, and it will be yours" (Mark 11:24).

> Prayer is not preparation for the battle. Prayer *is* the battle.

Since I covered so much of this in my book *PUSH: Praise, Pray, Persist Until Something Happens...*, here I will only encourage you to get a copy of this book and see how you can engage Heaven's hot-line (Prayer) for your BREAKTHROUGH. There is power in prayer! When we prevail in prayer, the enemy is defeated, miracles happen, and people turn from victims into victors. If you want to overcome the obstacles of everyday life, then YOU MUST PRAY. For "It is God who arms US with strength, And makes OUR way perfect" (Psalm 18:32).

• THE POWER OF THE HOLY SPIRIT

We are commanded to "be continually filled with the Holy Spirit" (Ephesians 5:18). Just keeping this one command of the Lord is a major part of our spiritual warfare, and we will need to use all the other weapons to stay in this place. A person who is "filled with the Spirit" and has learned to be "led by the Spirit" can also receive and use the "gifts of the Holy Spirit." As I always say: "The Holy Spirit is the Chief Executive of the divine program on earth. He is the One in charge of the affairs of the kingdom of God on earth. He is behind every exploit in the Kingdom of God. He is our number one Helper in fulfilling our destiny. He is the Spirit of the Lord."

> *"There are different kinds of gifts, but the same Spirit distributes them. There are different kinds of service, but the same Lord. There are different kinds of working, but in all of them and in everyone it is the same God at work."*
> 1 Corinthians 12:4-6

Friend, God does not want you to be ignorant of the mighty gifts of the Holy Spirit in you. In times past Satan has even used theologians to cast doubt on the availability of these gifts, but praise God we are learning to pick them up again and use them.

> *"To one there is given through the Spirit a message of wisdom, to another a message of knowledge by means of the same Spirit, to another faith by the same Spirit, to another gifts of healing by that one Spirit, to another miraculous powers, to another prophecy, to another distinguishing between spirits, to another speaking in different kinds of tongues, and to still another the interpretation of tongues."*
> 1 Corinthians 12:8-10

Know your weapons

Most of these gifts are expressed through our mouths. They all operate through divine initiative. These specialised weapons – the gifts of the Holy Spirit – all work along with the other weapons of God to build up God's people, win people for Christ, and destroy the works of the devil. They all operate through faith.

> He is behind every exploit in the kingdom of God.

The Holy Spirit is the third person in the Trinity, which is made up of three distinct persons – God the Father, God the Son, God the Holy Spirit. The Holy Spirit is fully God. He is eternal, omniscient, omnipresent. He has a will and can speak. He is the comforter (John 14:25-26).

In fact, He is here to make life comfortable for God's children! So no matter what trials you may have to face on your way to the promised land, I pray that the Holy Spirit will help you to overcome and comfort you with the goodness of God.

• THE NAME OF JESUS

There's power in the name of Jesus! Most Christian prayers are uttered "in the name of Jesus." To many, this has come to be nothing more than a phrase that is little different from the farewell valediction at the close of a letter, such as "Sincerely yours." This is not a magic formula to be tacked onto the end of a prayer for effect. Of course we should pronounce the name of Jesus when we minister in God's name. The NAME OF JESUS is the AUTHORITY we have

THE PATH TO VICTORY

as we submit to Jesus Christ. We need to do what we are doing for the cause of Christ. There is no place for neutrality. We must do all that we do for Jesus, in Jesus, with Jesus.

When you fully submit to Jesus Christ and obey the Holy Spirit, God will back you up. You become the physical body of Christ for the situation. Demons will be forced to leave, even violently at times, as you have faith in the name of Jesus. He is there with you to back you up and make it happen! Today, submit yourself to God so you can resist the devil and he will flee from you (James 4:7).

MORE POWERFUL KEYS (WEAPONS) AND STRATEGIES FOR ACHIEVING THE VICTORY

- **The Blood of Jesus** (Revelation 12:10-11)

- **Fasting** (Matt 6:17-18)

- **Walking in obedience and consecration**
  (1 Samuel 15:22, 2 Chronicles 7:13-15)

- **Speaking in tongues** (1 Corinthians 14:2-4)

- **Your testimony** (Revelation 12:11)

- **Giving** (Malachi 3:10-11)

- **Walking in humility and submission**
  (Psalm 37:11, James 4:7)

STEP 6

Take a Step of Faith

"Then Joshua commanded the officers of the people, saying, "Pass through the camp and command the people, saying, 'Prepare provisions for yourselves, for within three days you will cross over this Jordan, to go in to possess the land which the Lord your God is giving you to possess."

Joshua 1:10-11

This great host of Israelites were about to embark on an untrodden path. Truly they had never passed this way before. They had never crossed the river Jordan (Joshua 3:4). Only two of this great number had even seen the river before (to our knowledge) when they crossed over to spy out the land. They were mighty swimmers aided by God in their quest to cross the mighty river. A hard task confronted them. In human terms and conditions, it was an impossible task. Beyond the Jordan was a mighty city to subdue.

The land they were to take by faith was just before them. No doubt emotions were high as they stood on the banks of the mighty flowing Jordan River, the only thing standing between the Israelites and the land God had promised them. There were no bridges or fjords, and the river was in flood. Crossing over safely was an apparently impossible obstacle. But God had given them a command and a promise.

THE PATH TO VICTORY

— **A Command:** "When you reach the edge of the Jordan's waters, go and stand in the river" (Joshua 3:8).

— **A Promise:** "…As soon as the priests who carry the ark of the Lord…set foot in the Jordan, its waters flowing downstream will be cut off and stand up in a heap" (Joshua 3:13).

The order in which these are given is very important: the command precedes the promise because it is obedience to the command that activates the promise.

> *"…As soon as the priests who carried the ark reached the Jordan and their feet touched the water's edge, the water from upstream stopped flowing"*
> Joshua 3:15-16a

Have you ever watched a child taking his or her first step? Do you remember the first time you were able to ride a bike without training wheels? As these events take place, excitement comes over you. An unexplainable joy fills the parents as they watch and smile or perhaps shed a tear of joy. But on the face of the one taking that first step you see fear and adventure. When the task is achieved you may see confusion and joy combined on that little face as the truth dawns: "I did it!" And then as that next step is taken you will hear laughter and joy. These are steps of Faith.

Faith is reaching out into the unknown and grasping onto it. Faith believes without seeing. Faith trusts when there is no reason to trust. That belief in faith is the core of who you are. It is important to note that before the river stopped the Israelites had to take the first step. The miracle

Take a step of faith

(the promise) did not begin until they took the first step (the command).

How much easier it would have been for them had God simply stopped the water from flowing *before* they got to the river or maybe at least before they took the first step into the raging river. That is not how it works. They had to literally take the first step in faith before anything miraculous happened. For me the first step is always the hardest, the riskiest, but also the most important one. Living out your faith is mostly in the first step.

> 𝔣𝔞𝔦𝔱𝔥 trusts 𝔴𝔥𝔢𝔫 𝔱𝔥𝔢𝔯𝔢 𝔦𝔰 no 𝔯𝔢𝔞𝔰𝔬𝔫 to 𝔱𝔯𝔲𝔰𝔱.

For Christians today crossing the Jordan represents passing from one level of the Christian life to another. It is not a picture of a believer dying and entering Heaven. Canaan (the promised land) was not Heaven but rather a place that had to be won by hard work. Entering Canaan is a picture not of entering into Heaven but rather of entering into spiritual warfare to claim what God has promised. Joshua understood the principle of faith. IF GOD SAID IT, IT COULD BE DONE! Nothing was impossible with Joshua's God.

To Joshua, Jericho was not a walled city but a wonderful way to display God's great power. The Jordan wasn't an obstacle but an opportunity to show Israel how God was going to take care of them in the promised land. They went over on dry ground. Every step in the Jordan was a miracle of God's provision and presence. That is why God had them cross in the season when the Jordan River flooded and overflowed its banks. God loves big obstacles to prove His power.

THE PATH TO VICTORY

Someone has said, "If the challenge is over your head and too great for you to do, it is probably God." Goliath stood high over David's head and looked down with distain, offended that Israel would send out a child to fight their battle. He was insulted by the audacity of his opponent. But anointed children are greater than any giant demon in the universe! Daniel slept with lions, which had a reputation of eating men for lunch. The fiery furnace was heated seven times its normal temperature for Israel's three testimonies of courage.

YOU ARE GREATER THAN ANY DEMON! Why? Because you are anointed and appointed by the GREAT I AM (GOD). Today, I encourage you to take a step of faith. For without faith it is impossible to please God (Hebrews 11:6). If you want to see what God can do for you, I challenge you to take a step out and walk with Christ. God responds to those who step out of the boat like Peter who walked on water (Matthew 14:22-33)

The Lord said, "Step out and walk, walk in faith and a path will open unto you!" In the case of the Israelites' crossing the Red Sea, the Red Sea was not opened all the way to the bank on the other side. The waters parted only as they walked out in faith. Step by step, the path to the other bank began to open unto them. (See Exodus 14.) Note that the people were not required to part and dry the sea. They were simply required to believe God's Word and to step in the direction of obedience. God did the rest.

> Step out and walk, walk in faith and a path will open unto you!

Throughout the Scriptures believers in various situations were faced with impossible challe-

Take a step of faith

nges. Think of David and Goliath or Daniel's three friends and the fiery furnace. Or think of the apostles in those early days in Jerusalem. They faced such massive opposition and threats of violence that it must have seemed impossible to some people that they could ever succeed. In all these impossible situations God's faithful people understood, believed, looked to God, and took steps in the direction of obedience. In each case, God did the rest.

Friend, God loves those who will challenge His faithfulness. He delights in proving how wonderful and powerful He really is. He wants you to trust Him and take a step of faith! Most people never experience the miracles of God because they prefer to stay in their comfort zone of complacency. That is why Jesus never said, "Sit ye" but rather "Go ye" (Matthew 26:18). God is a God of progress and adventure. Paul would have never visited the third heaven if he had not gone to Lystra and got stoned (2 Corinthians 12:1-10)!

Stepping out in faith and obedience releases the power of God. Whatever the impossible situation you may be facing, hear the Word and promise of God, focus on the Lord and His might, and determine the small steps of faith and obedience that will move you in the direction of the impossible. Then take that first step. If you will do just that much, God will take care of the rest.

STEP 7

EMBRACE GOD'S DIVINE STRATEGY

"Now Jericho was tightly shut up because of the Israelites. No one went out and no one came in. Then the Lord said to Joshua, "See, I have delivered Jericho into your hands, along with its king and its fighting men. March around the city once with all the armed men. Do this for six days. Have seven priests carry trumpets of rams' horns in front of the ark. On the seventh day, march around the city seven times, with the priests blowing the trumpets. When you hear them sound a long blast on the trumpets, have all the people give a loud shout; then the wall of the city will collapse and the people will go up, every man straight in." ...So the Lord was with Joshua, and his fame spread throughout the land. "

Joshua 6:1-5

To REACH THE NEXT LEVEL – the level of the breakthrough – we must do certain things. God said, "I have delivered Jericho into your hands." He did not say, "I will" but "I have." In other words, the deal was already done! The battle had already been won! The victory was guaranteed. All Joshua and the people had to do was OBEY!

Before Joshua launched his attack on Jericho, he had an encounter with a man bearing a drawn sword who identified himself as the "Commander of the army of the Lord" (Joshua 5:13-15). This Commander came with a message: "Take off your sandals, for the place where you

THE PATH TO VICTORY

are standing is holy." This experience reminds Joshua that the Lord God – not he himself – was the Commander-in-Chief. And since God was the Commander-in-Chief, He had specific instructions about the coming battle that He expected Joshua to obey.

When Joshua heard the instructions given in the verse above, he must have thought it was ridiculous: Have all the armed men follow seven trumpet-blowing priests stationed in front of the ark of the covenant as they march around Jericho once every day for six days and then, on the seventh day, repeat the process seven times ending the parade with a loud shout of all the people.

Wow! Just imagine yourself in Joshua's position. But Joshua knew that if the battle was to be the Lord's, then so the strategy must be the Lord's. Often when God (the Commander-in-Chief) provides a vision for what He wants to accomplish, He also provides a specific strategy for accomplishing it.

Remember that "the battle is not yours but the Lord's" (2 Chronicles 20:15). If you want to succeed and achieve victory, the Lord must be the One to fight the battle. The only way to take the promised land is to let the Lord fight the battle.

> God... the Commander-in-Chief

When God promises to be with us in our endeavors, He does not mean He is going to be cheerleading us from the bench, but rather that He will join us in the game as Team Captain and provide us with the strategies to win the game.

The key to success in any endeavor is listening to the captain in the field and doing as you are told. No matter what work you are engaged in, when the Lord is in it and

Embrace God's divine strategy

the strategies are from Him your secular work is transformed into spiritual ministry! God has a plan for your life (pre-planned from the foundation of the world) —a divine plan of victory!

> *"I know what I'm doing. I have it all planned out – plans to take care of you, not abandon you, plans to give you the future you hope for. When you call on me, when you come and pray to me, I'll listen. When you come looking for me, you'll find me. Yes, when you get serious about finding me and want it more than anything else, I'll make sure you won't be disappointed. GOD's Decree. I'll turn things around for you…."*
>
> Jeremiah 29:11-14, (The Message)

A few years back I came across the passage of scripture above, and it has revolutionized my faith and life. "GOD HAS A PLAN FOR MY LIFE." But I realized that there is a condition for me to walk in that pre-planned victory. God said in His Word, "When you come looking for Me, you will find Me. Yes, when you get serious about finding Me and want it more than anything else, I will make sure you won't be disappointed."

So I ask you: *How badly do you want victory? Is it worth it to you to deny yourself, take up your cross, and follow Jesus?* You need to get desperate for God and His ways. God wants you to love Him with all your heart, mind, and soul. When you are faithful in seeking Him and His plan for your life with all your heart, you open the doors of the divine for

THE PATH TO VICTORY

God to shower you with His faithfulness and blessing. And victory will come to your life in ever-increasing abundance. When you give up your will, you open the door for God's will and His perfect plan.

That means that you must surrender – give up – your will and actions that result from negative thoughts, insecurities, and personal fears about yourself. Don't be anxious about your life because God has it all planned out. A life of victory is only a quality decision away. So, then, the question remains: *Are you desperate enough to get serious about God and follow His path?* Remember: Narrow is the way that leads to life — *victorious life!*

God knows what He is doing. Just trust Him and embrace His divine strategy and stop pushing your own misguided agenda. God's purposes and plans will always prevail! Whatever you are doing, wherever you are going in life, "Trust in the Lord with all your heart and lean not on your own understanding; in all your ways acknowledge him, and he will make your paths straight" (Proverbs 3:5-6).

> God has a plan for your life.

Yes, God's riches are very great, and His wisdom and knowledge have no end! No one can explain the things God decides or understand His ways. As the Scripture says, "Who has known the mind of the Lord or been able to give him advice?" (Isaiah 40:13). "No one has ever given God anything that he must pay back" (Job 41:11).

Friend, when you allow your mind to understand this truth so that it manifests itself into your reality, you will know that the Lord is God. And when you learn to trust Him and lean and depend on Him, He will provide you with all that your heart desires. Beyond even that He will allow you to have a look into the future and see the possibi-

Embrace God's divine strategy

lities of what tomorrow will look like for all of those who can truly believe that all things are possible. If you can believe in your mind the things that God will show you and conceive them as being the manifestation of your current reality – right here and now – then you shall have them because truly they are yours.

God said, "You are now living in a time when everything around you seems to be happening instantly. Waiting on the vision that I have given you may seem like a dream that is never going to come true. You must know in your heart the truth of a thing when it is presented to you. Learn to stand on MY WORD *as never before* because MY WORD is truth, and when you come to a place in your life as a truth seeker, believing in the impossible, the truth will truly set your soul free." Understand this one truth: The revelation or

> God's purposes and plans will always prevail!

the vision from God is for an appointed time – a time that you may not comprehend, but know that it will hasten to the end and provide you with complete fulfillment. God's vision will not deceive you or disappoint you. It will take you to a place that you have never ever in your thoughts imagined you could go.

Brothers and sisters, it requires patience on your part to accept that God can never lie. And if He has spoken into your spirit a vision, a dream, a purpose, a strategy, or a plan, know this: He will bring it to reality because God *never ever* makes a promise He does not keep. All you need to do is:

- **Follow!** Focus on where God, by the Spirit, is leading you.

THE PATH TO VICTORY

- **Consecrate your life**, by renewing your commitment to Him, listening carefully for Him.
- **Move out!** Don't go just halfway toward the challenge and give in to the temptation to quit.
- **Memorialize!** Remember the victories and build your faith in the God who is at work in you today.

Let God cover you with His wings and bring you through your situation and carry you into life in all its abundant fullness. Yes, God knows what He's doing. God made all things and everything continues through Him and for Him. To Him be the glory forever! Amen!

Dear God,

"We want to thank You that You are not a Commander-in-Chief who simply delegates Your responsibility to us and leaves everything for us to decide — regarding the what, how, and when to do our job. Instead, we look to You to provide us with clear instructions to fight every battle we face on OUR way to victory. Through Christ our Lord, Amen!"

STEP 8

MAKE A JOYFUL NOISE!

"When the trumpets sounded, the people shouted, and at the sound of the trumpet, when the people gave a loud shout, the wall collapsed; so every man charged straight in, and they took the city."

Joshua 6:20

AFTER HEARING GOD'S COMMAND Joshua called his people and commanded them to advance and fight and destroy the enemy. God had commanded Joshua to attack Jericho. Jericho was the most well-protected and fortified city in all of Canaan. In the natural, sacking this mighty city seemed an impossible task! But God gave Joshua the promise of victory!

Let's look at Joshua 6. God promises Joshua that he will go in and possess Jericho —a shut up place. The name *Jericho* literally means "The Place of Fragrance." Fragrance was very significant in the Old Testament. In fact, God commanded that the priests burn incense in the Tabernacle because the fragrance of the incense symbolized prayer and praise going up before God.

What am I saying? Listen, Joshua and the people were about to go in and possess the place of fragrance! In other words, he was about to possess his praise. Right now, as you are reading this book, God wants you to possess "The Place Of Fragrance"! He wants you to possess your place of praise! He wants you to possess your place of prayer!

THE PATH TO VICTORY

The Bible declares:

> *"Let my prayer be set before You as incense, the lifting up of my hands as the evening sacrifice...."*
> Psalm 141:2

The place of your praise and worship has walls around it! There are walls of pride, walls of disobedience, walls of tradition, walls of ignorance, walls of fear! That is why you are very comfortable where you are, singing songs of religious super-spiritual praise. But God is calling you to break through the walls of your comfort zone, to break out of your well-protected religious practices! He wants you to go into the place of fragrance: That place of true praise!

Joshua needed a breakthrough! The Bible says he called together the priests and told them, "Take up the ark of the covenant of the Lord and have seven priests carry trumpets in front of it." He ordered the people to "Advance and march around the city, with the armed guard going ahead of the ark of the Lord." Quietly going around the city one time each day didn't exactly look like destroying the fortress of Jericho.

But the army of Israel had fully prepared themselves through circumcision. Their hearts were full of strength and a sense of victory. This was the strategy for paralyzing their enemies in fear.

Joshua spoke to the people. Then the seven priests carrying the seven trumpets went forward blowing the trumpets before the Lord with the ark of the Lord's covenant, which represents the very PRESENCE of God, following them. The armed guard marched ahead of the priests who blew the trumpets, and the rear guard followed

Make a joyful noise!

the ark. The whole time the trumpets were sounding, but Joshua had commanded, "Do not give a war cry, do not raise your voices, do not say a word until the day I tell you to shout. Then shout!"

The army of Israel under Joshua's command obeyed the command Joshua had given them *absolutely*. They did only and everything they were instructed to do.

> God is calling you to break through the walls of your comfort zone!

Just as General Joshua had commanded, they advanced softly, lightly stepping around the city of Jericho. And then the army of Israel returned to the camp and spent the night there. One thing is very clear: They won the victory by going around the city of Jericho in silence. Silence was their prayer. They acted as one man. The steadfast obedience of the army of Israel in faithfully executing their commander's orders and controlling their mouths imply that they had already won the war.

But on the seventh day, something happened. They got up earlier and circled the city seven times. Here's what Joshua and his army did after they circled the city for the seventh time on the seventh day:

> *"When the trumpets sounded, the people shouted, and at the sound of the trumpet, when the people gave a loud shout, the wall collapsed; so every man charged straight in, and they took the city."*
> Joshua 6:20

God brought a great victory to Joshua and the people of Israel. The Jericho fortress finally and completely collapsed to the ground. The soldiers of Israel were empowered by the Spirit of God. *Wow!* There was something in their shout that struck fear in their enemy! When the enemy heard them shouting like champions, they realized that the Israelites had faith in a God who was unbeatable.

Today is your day of a shout! The kingdom you are about to possess has shut you out for too long. Your family and your troubles have painted a somewhat difficult picture of victory. The Lord stirred me today to dare you to shout! Why? Because a shout is a symbol of dominion. *"When the people gave a loud shout, the wall collapsed."* When you give God a shout, He shakes the heavens and earth for your sake. God is your only audience, so take a break and tell your trouble, tell your family, tell your situation, tell your concerns, "I am going to give God a shout," and then just you watch as He deals with your giants.

> Today is your day of a shout!

I am here to announce to you that God is about to move on your behalf! He is about to give you a breakthrough in your WORSHIP and PRAISE! Though your walls have been shut up, it is time to possess your praise! It is time to take possession of your Canaan! Make a joyful noise to the Lord! And right now, wherever you are and whatever you are going through, give Him a praise for the victory!

God wants us to step out! He wants to take each of us to a new level where we can possess the LAND that He has given US. BUT first we need:

Obedience

In spite of all those accomplishments, Joshua's greatest attribute was his obedience to God. Joshua succeeded because he obeyed. He led the people of Israel to conquer the land because he was willing to follow God. If you want to make your life better, you must become a person of obedience. You will achieve nothing without obedience. Living in obedience to the Word of God does not happen automatically. It is a matter of the will, a matter of continual choice. Having the *desire* to be what God wants you to be and to do what He wants you to do is good, but you must take action! Translate that desire into devotion and that belief into behaviour! Set your will to seek Him and obey Him. The Apostle John tells us that to truly love God is to do His commandments.

> *"This is love for God: to obey his commands. And his commands are not burdensome."*
> 1 John 5:3

Though we often make obedience to God something difficult and complicated, it really isn't. In fact, it is very simple – as simple as: DO AS YOU ARE TOLD! Joshua could have done anything he wanted to do and he would have had the full support of the people. But Joshua refused to take advantage of the situation. Instead, he was completely obedient to the instruction from God.

Today, declare as the Psalmist did: "I will walk about in freedom, for I have sought your precepts" (Psalm 119:45). Friend, if you will only put your trust in God and follow the instructions of the God of battles then you will emerge victorious in each battle of life. God can be trusted to give you success strategies because He sees life from a perfect vantage point and His resources are unlimited. All He requires of you is prompt obedience, total co-operation, and a trusting heart.

Patience

Patience is the second thing you will need to possess your promised land. The Jericho Operation required great patience on the part of the people of Israel. It was not easy for them to march around the city for seven days without doing anything. They wanted to attack the city right away. Seven days must have seemed like seven long years to them. They wanted to rush to the city when they saw their enemies. But God told them to march around the city *silently*.

They were tired of the waiting game. One day passed and they waited. Two days passed and they waited. Six days passed and nothing happened. But they continued doing as they were told and they marched. Seven days passed and they waited. God wanted them to wait for *God's* time. When God's time came, they shouted and the wall collapsed.

> I am here to announce to you that God is about to move on your behalf!

Patience is essential if the promises of God are going to bear a fruitful harvest in our lives. In the parable of the sower, Jesus said, "But the ones that fell on the good ground are those who, having heard the word with a noble and good heart, keep it and bear fruit with patience" (Luke 8:15). God has promised that His word will bear fruit if we will but keep it patiently. Faith must not fade, and patience keeps it alive even in the midst of trials.

If you maintain your faith by patience, you will bear

good fruit. In Galatians 6:9 the Apostle Paul writes, "Let us not become weary in well-doing, for the proper time" – which is at God's appointed time, not our convenient time – "we will reap a harvest if we do not give up." This verse tells us that an impatient person who grows weary of waiting will display a fruitless faith and produce no spiritual harvest.

How much has been lost in the kingdom of God because God's people lacked patience? Many times in our lives we come face to face with various difficult situations. We stand at the crossroads of life wondering which direction we should take. At this junction, the crossroads offers us an opportunity to make a life-changing decision that will most certainly affect the rest of our lives.

So once again we ask ourselves: "Which direction should I take?" Our thoughts begin to take us on the journey that we initially set out to experience. As our minds begin to roam in the great distance, our patience begins to wear thin. We question ourselves again and ask: "Why have I been led to this point?" We see through a glass darkly, and if we are not careful the world, the flesh, and the devil will begin to stir doubts within us. Our doubts and not knowing often bring fear, which fills us with anxieties that cause us to forget that God has our backs and led us to this crossroads in order to teach us the patience we need to carry us through to our destination.

> *If you maintain your faith by patience, you will bear good fruit.*

At this point, we need patience to grow within us. Hebrews 10:36 instructs us: *"Patient endurance is what you*

THE PATH TO VICTORY

need now, so that you will continue to do God's will. Then you will receive all that He has promised." In our spiritual struggle to be conformed to the nature of Christ and advance His kingdom, faith and patience are the 1-2 punch that knock out the schemes of the enemy and bring us into the promised place of victory!

If you want to be all you were created to be and have all that the Lord has promised to give you, then you must "imitate those who through faith and patience inherit the promises" (Hebrews 6:12).

- **David** waited for God's time and endured many sufferings and Samuel anointed him to become the king of Israel.

- **Abraham** waited for 25 years to have Isaac, the son of God's promise.

- **Jacob** waited seven years to marry Rachel his beloved.

- **Simeon and Anna** in Luke 2 were waiting for the consolation of Israel and finally they saw the baby Jesus with their own eyes before they died.

- **The father of the prodigal son** in Luke 15 waited patiently for his dearly-loved run-away son. Finally, his lost son came home and the father welcomed him with arms of love.

You have to wait for God's time. You have come too far to let impatience thwart your God-given strategy to possess the promised land. Impatience is the opposite of patience, and is corrosive to true faith. Impatience is a grave threat to faith because the impatient man becomes weary and gives up. An impatient man may not say it, but his actions show that he believes that God should serve his own agenda. A patient man, on the other hand, can say to the Lord, "Not my will but Yours be done." An impatient man is restless and short-tempered, while a patient man is a disciple who denies himself daily and takes up his cross to follow Jesus.

I believe you are in the second group (patient disciples). A patient man bears pains and trials calmly and without complaint. He is steadfast and remains faithful, trusting God absolutely, despite opposition, difficulty, and adversity.

Impatience is a work of the flesh, whereas patience is a fruit of the Holy Spirit. Patience reflects God's very presence in our lives, for He is a patient and forbearing and longsuffering God. If He were not, we would all have been annihilated long ago! An impatient man is in a hurry and expects everything to go his way. But God is never in a hurry, and He expects His disciples to follow Him.

... Wait for God's time.

We are to be still before the Lord without fretting. We are to wait patiently for His instruction and His direction. One of the greatest stresses in life is this stress of waiting for God, but Isaiah assures us that "those who wait for the Lord will gain new strength; they will mount up with wings like eagles, they will run and not get tired, they will walk and not become weary" (Isaiah 40:31). Those who willingly wait for the Lord glisten like gemstones in the eyes of God. *Wow!!!*

Most people, however, see the very thought of waiting

THE PATH TO VICTORY

as a torturous frustration that must be tolerated only if it cannot be avoided. In our society, we avoid the word "wait" like a contagious disease. We no longer even use the phrase "waiting room." In offices, it is called the "reception room" or the "front desk" and in hospitals it is referred to as "the "family area." We are an impatient people in an impatient culture.

One thing we can be sure of is that *God's time is always the right time.* His management of our situations is always the best management. Patience is not learning to wait for others; it is learning to wait on God and to cooperate with His work in your life. Patience means awaiting God's time without doubting God's love.

Friend, the Lord is calling you to wait upon Him in confident trust. "Rest in the Lord, and wait patiently for Him" (Psalm 37:7). You are to wait with hope-filled anticipation. You are in the "waiting room of God," and as long as you wait you must be expectant. If you live your life as you are instructed in Psalm 37:7, waiting patiently for the Lord, you will find that He will give you what is best … in *His* time!

The Lord recently spoke this important prophetic word to a friend of mine: "Those who wait and watch will avoid worry, for patience prepares you for peace. Only through patience can you possess peace, and only those with perseverance will withstand persecution." Our good God knows that the end of the age will be a tumultuous time filled with persecution, but He wants us to be those who can withstand the persecution without fear and remain in perfect peace. The Spirit

> **We are to wait patiently for His instruction and His direction.**

of the Lord is exhorting the Bride to be adorned with the beauty of patience so that through faith and patience we will be able to stand against the onslaught of the enemy and receive every precious promise the Lord has given to us.

Praise God in advance

Praise always precedes the victory. Before you will see the victories in your life you must learn to give God the highest praise. As long as you remain focused on your problems, you will not experience victory because a problem-focus limits the things that God can do in your life.

Praise is your faith at work in your life; it is praise that will activate God's power in you. No matter what you are going through, you should *always* give God praise. If you really want to get God's attention, start giving Him praise and thanksgiving in advance for a breakthrough in the midst of a storm and see what happens.

Victory will happen to you just as it happened to the children of Israel when they obeyed God patiently and gave a loud shout on the seventh day! The Scripture says "the wall collapsed" and God brought a great victory to His people and delivered on His promise!

You may be at a place today where you have unborn promises. You keep praying for those loved ones … but aren't seeing the change. During times like these, it is tempting to give up and say, "Too bad. It's never going to happen." Don't you do it! Don't give in and make the devil's day! It is at just such times when you need to praise God even more. Don't give up! Because the joy of the Lord is your strength and He delights in your praise.

THE PATH TO VICTORY

Praise opens the door for God to move and for breakthroughs to come. Whenever you can offer up a sacrifice of praise when things don't look good, you can be assured that God is working in your life. You cannot keep a person who praises God down! Your praise will lead to victory. Declare God's victory in your life in praise even *before* you achieve your victories.

In this next season of your life, I want to challenge you. Why don't you put down your sword for a minute and just tap into the power of His joy. Release your praise to Him as a gift of love. Rejoice in who He is and in what He has given you. Get up every morning and tap into His joy. Pour out to the Lord in praise and thanksgiving and watch God turn circumstances from stormy to bright!

MAKE A SHOUT OF VICTORY! THE LAND IS YOURS!!!

CONCLUSION

Your path to victory

●●●●●●●●●●●●●●●●●●●

Conclusion

YOUR PATH TO VICTORY

You now have the eight simple, Bible-based steps that will take you to victory over any problem you may face.

1. Be strong and courageous

2. Define your territory!

3. Identify the obstacles

4. Stand! You are not alone

5. Know your weapons

6. Take a step of faith

7. Embrace God's divine strategy

8. Make a joyful noise!

These steps represent God's established order for successfully operating in faith. As we have seen over and over, divine order is a prerequisite for miracles. I pray that this book has provided you with a clear understanding about how to locate your destiny and given you the tools you need to possess the promised land and to fulfill all that God has called you to do. There is a preordained and speci-

THE PATH TO VICTORY

fic path God has designed for your life. It is up to you to discover it and choose to take that path.

Today you may be getting ready to have the door opened up for you to enter into your Promised Land — into God's true call on your life. You are well aware of the "giants" and "strongholds" you will have to face once this door opens for you. Remember that Joshua saw the same "giants" and "strongholds" that you are seeing. He saw all this before going in. God allowed him to see exactly what he was going into before he actually went into it. God is showing you the same thing.

You have a choice to make. You can either (A) let fear and panic set in just as the Israelites did before God vested Joshua with their leadership and lose your chance to enter into your "Promised Land" or (B) have the same strong faith and belief in God that Joshua had — and go in there with a "kick butt attitude" confident in God that you will be victorious and that you will accomplish everything that God wants you to accomplish.

I will leave you with one last thought. Joshua excercised his strong faith and belief in God and entered the Promised Land and achieved total victory in God. The Bible says God is "no respecter of persons." What He will do for one, He will do for another. If God is calling you to go through this door then TAKE A STEP OF FAITH and rest assured that you will have the full power of God operating through you to achieve total victory just as Joshua did!

Now, let's pray...

"Heavenly Father, I give You thanks and praise today for the promise of victory. I open my mind and heart to You. I receive

Your path to victory

Your Word, which directs my steps and builds my faith. Help me to hear Your voice clearly so that I can move confidently into the abundant life You have for me in Jesus' name. Amen!"

Thoughts & Reflections

≈≈≈

Thoughts & Reflections

≈≈≈

How Can You Know God's Will For Your Life?

Three Conditions:

1. Are you willing to do God's will BEFORE you know what it is?

2. Are you, right now, clean? Cleansed according to 1 John 1:9 (Spiritual Breathing). You cannot expect to know God's will if you are knowingly harboring unconfessed sin.

3. Are you surrendered — focused on Christ? (Filled with the Holy Spirit… according to Ephesians 5:18)?

Friend, If Christ is on the throne of your life right now, you are in the exact center of God's will for your life…because God's will is not a location or vocation…it is a relationship. When we stay in that relationship, the vocation or location issues work themselves out in many natural and supernatural ways!

We have covered some life-changing principles in this book. But the only way to walk in these principles is to have a living relationship with Jesus Christ. If you have never declare Jesus Christ as the Lord and Savior of your life, here is your chance.

God loves you and He has a great plan for your life. He sent Jesus to take your punishment for sin. He wants to know you better. He is in the fixing business of those who

THE PATH TO VICTORY

are lonely; have a broken heart; or are at the end of their ropes. If you will receive Him as Lord and Savior, all your sin will be forgiven instantly and you will become a new creation; your sin nature will die, and your spirit will come alive on the inside with the life of God and His righteousness.

I invite you to pray this prayer to God, from your heart.

Dear God I know I'm a sinner, I know I am not where I want to be, and I want Your forgiveness! I believe that Jesus died on the cross to pay the price for my sins. Please wash me clean from all sin, shame, and guilt, come into my life Jesus to be my Lord and Savior. Come and live in me; abide in me. I ask this in Your name Jesus. Amen!

Now, if you just prayed that prayer, you are a born-again Christian. Heaven is your eternal home, righteousness is your gift, the Holy Spirit is alive on the inside of you, and all your sins have been forgiving. Now you can walk in the righteousness of God. You are an overcomer! You are more than a conqueror! YOUR NAME IS VICTORY!!!

Thoughts & Reflections

Think About It

1. What is Divine Order?

_____

_____

_____

_____

_____

_____

2. How do you understand God's plan?

_____

_____

_____

_____

THE PATH TO VICTORY

_____

_____

_____

_____

_____

_____

3. What Is God's Plan for Your Life?

_____

_____

_____

_____

_____

_____

Thoughts & Reflections

4. Read Joshua 1:8. What do you notice about God's command to Joshua? Why is it significant?

5. What promises has God made you? Do you expect that He will keep them? If so, how does it change your approach to daily life? If not, why not, and what would you do differently if you did expect God to keep His promises?

_____

_____

_____

_____

_____

_____

_____

_____

_____

_____

Thoughts & Reflections

_____

_____

_____

_____

_____

_____

6. What are you declaring over your life?

_____

_____

_____

_____

_____

_____

7. As a believer, how can you overcome fear?

Thoughts & Reflections

8. What are the two keys given in 1 John 5:4 for overcoming the world?

9. If you are "more than a conqueror," how does the Bible command you to live?

_____

_____

_____

_____

_____

_____

_____

_____

_____

_____

BIBLIOGRAPHY

John Stevenson, *Joshua, Judges, And Ruth: Victory, Defeat, And Hope In An Age Of Heroes*, (Redeemer Publishing, 2008).

Taking The Land. www.actionevangelism.org

Christian Cheong, *Overcoming Obstacles*, Website – Blog, 2001.

The Lord is with you in the battle! (NNED series)

Michael, Fackerell. *Weapons of Our Warfare*. Website Blog, www.christian-faith.com, 2007.

Rupert Hankey, *Stepping out of faith*, (St Andrews, 2012)

Taking The Land (www.actionevangelism.org)

Pst. Branden, *Worship – The Key To Life*, (NBWC, 2011)

Jericho Operation (http://www.washingtonubf.org)

ABOUT THE AUTHOR

Determined, Innovative, Anointed, and Cutting Edge are some words often used to describe **JERRY BONSU.** Founder and Senior minister of **V**ictory Life International Center (VLIC), a revolutionary Movement of 'like minded' and 'like spirited' people coming together in one accord: whose mission is to empower and equip individuals through teaching and preaching the uncompromised Word of God, and helping them to fulfill their highest calling and usher them into a supernatural lifestyle of faith and abundant living.

Jerry is also the visionary and founder behind several entities, including: Victory in Praise International Gathering, a vibrant, dynamic worship conference, which brings together more than 2000 people each gathering, —a wide audience of pastors, worship leaders, artists, musicians, scholars, students, and other interested worshipers. Founder and President of Jerry Bonsu Ministries (JBM); Jerry is also the leader of a gospel group Jerry Bonsu & Levitical Anointing; And the co-founder of a non-profit organization Elyon Foundation, created to influence the next generation.

Jerry —dynamic conference speaker, author, life coach, entrepreneur, worship leader... also travels throughout the world with his breakthrough teaching on understanding your God-given identity, purpose, and destiny in Christ. His mission is to impact his generation with divine revelation. Jerry and his wife, Laetitia are the proud parents of two children, Janelle Kierra and Janessa Kimani.

PUSH

By Jerry Bonsu

Believing that God can take you safely through all of the storms of this life can be difficult. God's timing doesn't always line up with our way of doing things and it may seem that we are alone in our battles. The raging storms of life brings many questions: What do you do when you are facing a serious medical issue, a crumbling marriage, financial difficulty, an addiction or any overwhelming problem that just won't go away? How do you continue waiting on God especially when you are pregnant with purpose?

In PUSH, Jerry Bonsu shares practical truths about the power of Praise, Prayer and Persistence that will carry you to new and exciting heights of splendor, hope, and love that only the Master could design - especially for you. You'll gain insight into how you can learn to stand firmly and have lasting peace and confidence in the face of adversity.

AVAILABLE ON WWW.JERRYBONSU.ORG

Also on www.amazon.com

Books & CD's by Jerry Bonsu

* *PUSH*
* *The Power Of I AM*
* *The Power Of I AM (Audio Book)*
* *Victory Noise (Album)*

Order these inspiring products and more by visiting www.jerrybonsu.org and be sure to join this movement on Facebook & Twitter.

WWW.JERRYBONSU.ORG

www.ingramcontent.com/pod-product-compliance
Lightning Source LLC
Chambersburg PA
CBHW071309040426
42444CB00009B/1949